IMMIGRATION M

CAN'T AFFORD TO MAKE

*What you need to know to avoid common
immigration mistakes*

IMMIGRATION MISTAKES YOU CAN'T AFFORD TO MAKE

What you need to know to avoid common immigration mistakes

KIMBERLEY SCHAEFER
Attorney At Law

ISBN: 0983739102
ISBN-13: 978-0983739104

CONTENTS

INTRODUCTION

Thank you for buying or requesting this book.

This book is for you if you are interested in learning more about some of the immigration mistakes that people make that I see in my work as an immigration lawyer. This book does not attempt to cover every possible immigration mistake that people make or that I see. Instead, it gives a general overview of some of the common mistakes that people make.

I initially wrote this book to help people who were considering hiring me as their immigration lawyer get a better feel for whether I would be the best immigration lawyer for their case. But, I believe that this book can be helpful to anyone who is interested in learning more about some of the common immigration mistakes that people make. The book also includes information on how an immigration lawyer may be able to help you with your case and what you should keep in mind if you are considering hiring an immigration lawyer to represent you.

Please keep in mind that everyone's immigration situation is unique. Although this book provides an overview of some of the general immigration mistakes that I see as an immigration lawyer, it is not intended to be, and it is not, legal advice specific to your situation. You should seek the advice of an immigration lawyer to give you advice specific to your situation. It is my hope that this book will help you better understand the complexity of immigration law so that you can better understand how an immigration lawyer can help you and when you should consult with an immigration lawyer.

DISCLAIMER

This book is not intended to be, and it is not, legal advice. The information in this book is general in nature and cannot be relied upon as legal advice related to your particular situation.

Every effort was made to ensure that the information presented in this book was accurate at the time it was written. However, because immigration law changes on a frequent basis, there is no guarantee that this information will remain accurate. Further, in many cases even small changes in facts can lead to significantly different outcomes in immigration related matters and this book is not intended to cover every possible factual situation. You should not rely on the information in this book when making decisions about your specific immigration situation. If you need legal or other expert assistance, you should consult with an immigration lawyer about your specific situation.

This book does not create an attorney-client relationship between you and the Schaefer Law Firm or Kimberley Schaefer. Only a written client representation signed by both you and Kimberley Schaefer creates an attorney-client relationship between you and Kimberley Schaefer or the Schaefer Law Firm.

CONSEQUENCES OF IMMIGRATION MISTAKES

Immigration law is a very complex and challenging area of law. Mistakes made in relation to immigration matters can have devastating consequences. Those consequences can include:

--- Denied immigration petitions that result in the inability of families to reunite.

--- Denied immigration petitions that result in families being separated for significantly longer times than necessary.

--- The loss of initial filing fees, sometimes in the amount of thousands of dollars.

--- The extra expense of having to pay additional fees to appeal a negative decision or to refile an application.

--- Being placed in removal proceedings or being deported from the United States.

--- Being unable to enter or re-enter the United States.

--- The inability to become a permanent resident of the United States or the inability to become a United States citizen.

The first step to avoiding costly immigration mistakes is to educate yourself before you move forward with your immigration case. Even "simple" immigration matters can become very complex and mistakes related to "simple" immigration matters can have devastating results. By educating yourself before speaking with an immigration lawyer about your case, you will have a better idea of the questions you should ask your lawyer and how your lawyer can help you.

Even if you have a friend who was successful in an immigration matter similar to yours, you may not have the same result. One reason you may not get the same result is because there are frequent changes to immigration law and the law may have changed since your friend's case. You cannot rely on what someone else has done in the past to be your guide in what you should do with your current immigration case because:

> --- the options that were available to others may not be available to you;

> --- you may have new options available to you that others in the past did not have; and

> --- small changes in your factual situation can lead to significantly different outcomes.

Failing to take into account the above factors could lead you to unknowingly take steps that lead to costly consequences such as those mentioned above.

This book is intended to give you an overview of some of the immigration mistakes that I see in my work as an immigration lawyer. This book does not cover every possible mistake that people make related to immigration law. My hope is that this book will provide you useful general information that will help you understand the complexity of immigration law and the role that an immigration lawyer can play in helping you avoid costly immigration mistakes.

❖ ❖ ❖

IMMIGRATION MISTAKES YOU CAN'T AFFORD TO MAKE

Immigration Mistake 1
Applying for an immigration benefit when you don't qualify.

Each year many people apply for immigration benefits for which they are not qualified. This typically happens when people simply don't realize that they don't meet all of the requirements for the immigration benefit in question, or they incorrectly assume that because a friend was successful with a similar application that they will also be successful. Three areas where this mistake can be particularly devastating are adjustment of status applications, asylum applications and naturalization applications.

Adjustment of status applications involve applying for permanent resident status when you are already in the United States. These applications are often based on family relationships and, if successful, allow you to become a permanent resident and obtain a green card without first having to return to your home country for an interview at the embassy or consulate. Not everyone qualifies for adjustment of status. For example, most people who entered the United States illegally will not be eligible for adjustment of status. If you don't qualify for adjustment of status but submit an application anyway, you will likely find yourself in deportation proceedings.

There are also very specific requirements for filing an asylum application. Generally speaking, you need to file an asylum application within one year of your last entry to the United States unless you qualify for an exception to this rule. If you aren't qualified for asylum because you apply more than one year after your entry to the United States and don't qualify for an exception to the one year rule, you will likely be placed in removal proceedings if you are not in a lawful immigration status.

Applying for naturalization when you aren't qualified can also cause serious immigration consequences. For example, if you don't qualify to become a citizen due to criminal convictions, your naturalization application will bring your convictions to the attention of immigration officials and you may find yourself fighting deportation in immigration court. With this in mind, if you have any criminal convictions you should seriously consider consulting with an immigration lawyer before you file a naturalization application.

Immigration Mistake 2
Thinking that you can save money by handling your immigration case on your own without a lawyer and then hiring a lawyer for the appeal if you lose.

Immigration matters can be very expensive. In addition to the required government filing fees (which could total into the thousands of dollars), you may also have to pay additional costs such as translation costs and medical exam fees. Some cases will also require expert witnesses to testify about country conditions, costs associated with psychological evaluations to help show hardship factors or DNA tests to prove family relationships.

With all of these expenses, it can be very tempting to try to save money by not hiring a lawyer to represent you. Often people believe that they can simply try to do their case on their own and will hire a lawyer if they are not successful so the lawyer can handle the appeal for them. This is a very risky strategy for several reasons.

First, this approach could result in added filing fee costs. Depending on the situation you may find that appealing your case may involve expensive filing fees in order to file the forms to appeal a negative decision. Other situations may require you to pay the initial filing fees a second time.

In addition, you may find that if your case involves a short deadline for filing an appeal that you will not be able to find an immigration lawyer who can take your case on short notice or that you will be charged a premium because the lawyer will have to work quickly to meet the deadline.

In some situations, it simply may not be possible for an immigration lawyer to build a strong case on appeal. For example, when you appeal an immigration court decision, in most cases you can only use in the appeal the evidence that was submitted during the original case. Therefore, if you lost your original case because you did not submit to the court the evidence needed to win your case, it may not be possible for an immigration lawyer to use that evidence to win your case on appeal.

Immigration Mistake 3
"My friend won and didn't have a lawyer, so I'll just do what they did."

It can be very tempting to try to save on legal fees by simply copying a friend's successful application. This is a very risky strategy for three reasons:

> --- Even small changes in facts can make a very big difference in the outcome of immigration cases. Your friend's case may appear to be almost like yours, but that doesn't mean you'll have the same outcome if you copy what they did.

> --- Changes in the law may mean that the option your friend had is no longer available.

--- Changes in the law may mean that you have better options available to you than your friend had available.

What could be the consequences of following this strategy? Depending on the situation, you could end up applying for an immigration benefit for which you don't qualify or that no longer exists. If this happens, not only will your application be denied, but you could end up being placed in deportation proceedings. You also could end up losing your application fee, which is some cases can run over a thousand dollars. If there are better options available to you, you could miss out on those options because you didn't know that they existed. Never simply rely on what a friend did in their case --- always verify the rules and regulations related to the current immigration law.

Immigration Mistake 4
Misrepresenting facts or submitting fraudulent documents because "they'll never find out" or because you are afraid of being denied.

It is not uncommon for me to see cases where someone is facing a difficult immigration situation because of an earlier misrepresentation on an immigration form or to an immigration officer. This often happens because the person:

--- misunderstood the question that was being asked;

--- was afraid to tell the truth because they thought that they would be denied if they gave the honest answer; or

--- were advised by someone that they needed to submit certain types of documents in order to win their case and decided that it would be better to submit fraudulent documents than nothing at all.

All of the above cause needless immigration problems that can easily be avoided. You should never misrepresent facts on an immigration form or to an immigration officer. You should never submit fraudulent documents with an immigration form or to an immigration officer. Do not listen to anyone who tells you to do so. Even if the facts of your situation will make it challenging to win your case, an immigration lawyer may be able to find a way to win your case or find an exception that will work in your favor. But, if you add the complication of a misrepresentation or fraudulent documents to your case, it will be much more unlikely that an immigration lawyer can find a solution to your immigration issue.

In particular, the consequences of misrepresentations or submitting fraudulent documents can be devastating. Not only will the misrepresentation likely cause your application to be denied, but you will likely have to address the misrepresentation in any future applications --- even if you reapply many years in the future. Depending on the situation, you may be required to apply for a waiver in order to be eligible for future immigration benefits. Waivers for misrepresentations can be very difficult to win.

If you have made a misrepresentation or submitted fraudulent documents in the past, you should let your immigration lawyer know about what happened. If your immigration lawyer knows what happened, it may be possible to find a way to overcome what happened in the past. Your lawyer can't help you overcome this issue if your lawyer doesn't know what happened.

Immigration Mistake 5
Not showing up for an immigration court hearing or showing up late.

If you are in immigration court proceedings, it is very important that you show up on time for every hearing. Not attending your hearing or not showing up on time will likely cause you to be ordered removed even though you may not have had the opportunity to present your case to the immigration judge. It can be very difficult, if not impossible, to fix this situation.

You should plan ahead for your immigration court hearing. Because transportation problems are not a valid excuse for missing your hearing, you should consider the following:

> --- If you have never been to the immigration court before, you should go to the court before your hearing. Make sure that you go during a time of day that will give you a similar traffic pattern to what you will face when you go for your hearing.

> --- If you will be driving to the hearing, make sure that you know where you plan to park and have a plan for what you will do if your planned parking lot is full.

> --- If a friend will be driving you to your hearing, make sure that they know how important it is that they pick you up on time so that you get to the court on time.

> --- If you plan on taking public transportation, make sure you allow plenty of time in case the bus or train is running late. You should also have a plan in place in case public transportation is not running for some reason.

> --- If your hearing is in the winter, you should also plan ahead in case there is snow or ice on the roads.

> --- Assume that there will be a traffic accident or traffic jam that causes a delay and plan to leave your house early just in case the drive takes longer than you planned.

--- Plan extra time for getting through the security line at the immigration court.

--- You may want to see if there is a restaurant or park nearby where you could eat breakfast or lunch before your hearing. Planning on eating near the court before your hearing will help you build extra time into your schedule to make sure that you get to your hearing on time. If your commute takes longer than you expected, you can always skip breakfast or lunch and go directly to the court.

Immigration Mistake 6
Missing a filing deadline.

There is very little forgiveness in immigration law for missing a filing deadline. You should always carefully check the filing deadlines for your case. Never wait until the last minute to file an immigration form, because the consequences of missing a deadline can be devastating.

For example, when appealing a case to the Board of Immigration Appeals, you should carefully note the filing deadline. Your notice of appeal or brief must arrive at the Board of Immigration Appeals on or before the deadline. It isn't enough for you to mail your package on the last day. It must arrive before the deadline. If your package is delayed due to bad weather or the error of the delivery service or post office, your package will still be considered to have been filed late. A late filed notice of appeal or brief may mean that you automatically lose your appeal.

If you have been asked to respond to a Request for Evidence (RFE) by mail, you should also be very careful to meet the filing deadline listed in the RFE. If you don't submit the requested documents in time, your petition or application may be denied. This can be particularly devastating when dealing with petitions that have a very long waiting time for approval.

For example, immigrant visa petitions for brothers or sisters can take over ten years for final approval. You don't want to be in a position where you waited for ten years and then missed a filing deadline by a day causing you to have to start over with a new ten year wait. Failing to meet the RFE deadline for an adjustment of status application can result in your application being denied and you could be sent to immigration court. It is far less stressful and much less expensive to meet the filing deadline than to have to fight your case in immigration court.

To avoid these harsh consequences, you should always mail your package with plenty of time for it to arrive at the correct office. For appeals to the Board of Immigration Appeals, you may want to consider using a filing service. These services are typically law firms with offices that are close to the Board of Immigration Appeals. For a fee you will be able to fax or email your package to the filing service and they will print it out and personally deliver it to the Board of Immigration Appeals for you, often on the same day you send it to them.

Immigration Mistake 7
Not understanding the possible immigration consequences before going into criminal court or entering into a plea bargain.

The immigration consequences of a criminal conviction can be very serious. Depending on the type of conviction, you could be deported from the United States and may never be able to return. Depending on the nature of the conviction, you may not be eligible for many forms of relief from deportation. Even misdemeanor convictions or alternative sentencing or diversion programs can result in these harsh consequences.

Key things you should keep in mind if you are facing criminal charges and are not a citizen:

--- Always make sure that your criminal defense lawyer knows that you are not a citizen. Your criminal defense lawyer can't help you avoid the immigration consequences of a possible conviction if he doesn't know that he needs to protect your immigration status.

--- Make sure that your criminal defense lawyer keeps the possible immigration consequences in mind when negotiating any plea agreement. A plea agreement that minimizes the time you spend in jail may not be the best one for you if it also means that you will be deported from the United States.

--- Even misdemeanor convictions can result in very harsh immigration consequences. It is even possible for a conviction that is considered to be a misdemeanor by the state to be viewed as an aggravated felony for immigration purposes. You should take every criminal charge seriously even if it is a misdemeanor charge.

--- Depending on your situation, if you are detained by the state you may also have what is called an immigration detainer placed on you. This means that even if you post bond in your criminal case, you may not be released from jail because you have an immigration hold placed on you. Always confirm whether you have an immigration detainer before posting bond in your criminal case.

--- Be very careful when someone advises you that you won't need to worry about the criminal charge because you can get the conviction expunged or you will be eligible for some sort of alternative sentencing or diversion program. Although these programs may help you keep your criminal record clear, many of them will not solve the immigration consequences of the conviction and you may still be deported. Always verify whether these types of programs will protect your immigration status as well as protect your criminal record.

Immigration Mistake 8
Traveling overseas when you may be inadmissible because of a criminal conviction or some other reason.

If you have any type of criminal conviction, you should always verify before you travel outside the United States whether your conviction will make you inadmissible to the United States. If it does, you risk not being allowed to return to the United States, being place in immigration detention upon your return or being sent to immigration court for removal proceedings.

It is not uncommon for people to think that it is safe to travel outside the United States if they have an old conviction or if they have safely traveled in the past after a criminal conviction. They are then shocked when they try to reenter the United States and are placed in immigration detention or sent to immigration court. Even old convictions can result in these harsh consequences because as more criminal records become centralized, it is becoming more likely that your criminal record will be noticed upon your return to the United States, even if it wasn't noticed in the past.

Many people think that if they were only convicted of a misdemeanor then they can safely travel. This is not necessarily true. Many misdemeanor convictions will make you inadmissible to the United States. Some misdemeanor convictions will even be considered to be aggravated felonies for immigration purposes. If this is true in your case, that means that you would have very limited immigration options available to you and you may have to fight your case in immigration court while you are in immigration detention. Immigration detention centers are basically jails --- you don't want to risk having to fight your immigration case while you are stuck in jail.

Other people incorrectly believe that the diversion program they were given or the expungement of their conviction means that they can safely travel. Although these problems may help you keep your criminal record clean, many of these programs do not solve the possible immigration consequences that you may face.

Immigration Mistake 9
Going to visit a friend or family member in immigration detention without verifying they are still at that detention center.

Many people who have a friend or family member who is detained in an immigration detention center want to be able to visit. You can do an initial check on which detention center the person is at by using the online detainee locator system found at:

https://locator.ice.gov/odls/homePage.do

To use this system, you will either need (1) the person's A-number and country of birth, or (2) the person's first name, last name, country of birth and date of birth.

Many immigration detention centers are located in remote locations. In addition, many people are transferred to immigration detention centers that are far from their homes, often with short notice. Before you go to visit a person in an immigration detention center, you should always verify that the person you are going to visit is still at the immigration detention center and hasn't been transferred. This is particularly true if you live a long distance from the detention center.

When you call the detention center to verify that the person you are going to visit is still there, you should also confirm the visiting hours and any special rules that the detention center has for visitors. It is not uncommon for there to be limited visitation hours, and in some cases there may be no weekend visitation hours available. In addition, there will likely be limits on what you can bring into the detention center and whether children are allowed to visit. Verifying this information before you go to visit will help you avoid the frustration of traveling for hours only to not be able to see your family member or friend.

Immigration Mistake 10
Accepting voluntary departure and then not leaving the United States within the allowed time.

In some circumstances, a person who is placed in removal proceedings can request what is called voluntary departure. If granted, voluntary departure allows the person to voluntarily leave the United States at their own expense instead of being deported by the government. Voluntary departure can make it easier to return to the United States in the future.

However, you should not accept voluntary departure unless you are positive that you will leave the United States within the time that the immigration judge gives you. If you don't leave the United States in the time given to you, you could be fined up to $5,000 and will be ineligible for many forms of immigration benefits for a period of ten years. This means that if you remain in the United States you would not be able to apply for adjustment of status to obtain a green card for ten years. Even after the ten year period, you would have to file a successful motion to reopen your immigration court case before you could apply for adjustment of status.

Before accepting voluntary departure, you should make sure that you understand the consequences of failing to leave the United States on time. You should also keep in mind that voluntary departure will avoid the consequences of a removal order, but will not solve other grounds of inadmissibility such as the 10-year bar for being unlawfully present in the United States for more than one year. If you aren't sure if voluntary departure is right for you or whether you may have other options available to you, you should consult with an immigration lawyer before your immigration court hearing.

Immigration Mistake 11
Assuming that you don't qualify for asylum because you have never been politically active.

Many people are familiar with the phrase "political asylum" and think that you can only get asylum if you are politically active. You can receive asylum if you would face persecution in your home country on account of your political beliefs. You can also receive asylum based on your race, religion, nationality or membership in a particular social group.

To qualify for asylum, you must show past persecution or a well-founded fear of future persecution on account of your race, religion, nationality, membership in a particular social group or political opinion. These categories cover many possible situations, especially the category of membership in a particular social group. Among other things, a particular social group could be based on family ties, tribal or clan membership, being a victim of female circumcision (also called female genital mutilation or female genital cutting), or being a victim of domestic violence.

Although these categories cover many situations, not everyone who faces the risk of harm or persecution in their home country will qualify for asylum. It is not enough for you to have a fear of persecution --- your fear must be of persecution on account of one of the five protected grounds mentioned above. In addition, you must be able to describe your situation and present evidence that proves that the persecution you would face is on account of one of these protected grounds. Because making this type of legal argument can be very complicated, I strongly recommend that you consult with an immigration lawyer before you file an asylum application.

There are many other things that you may need to show in order for your asylum application to be approved. For example, if you suffered past persecution you should be prepared to show that the situation in your home country has not improved and that you can't simply relocate to another part of your country. An immigration lawyer can help you identify all of the things you need to be able to prove to win your asylum case and can help you identify and collect the evidence needed to win your case. If you do not plan on working with an immigration lawyer, you should plan on spending a considerable amount of time studying asylum law so that you can learn what is needed to win your case.

Immigration Mistake 12
Sending immigration forms to the wrong address or without the correct filing fee.

Sending immigration forms to the wrong address or without the correct filing fee is a common mistake. To avoid this mistake, you should always verify the correct mailing address and fee by going to the USCIS website at:

http://www.uscis.gov

The USCIS website will have up-to-date information on the correct mailing addresses and filing fees. You should make sure that you include in your package the fees for each form you are submitting and any biometrics fee that is required.

If you don't send your immigration forms to the correct address or don't include the correct filing fees, your package will be rejected. Depending on the situation, you may be able to correct the problem by resubmitting the entire package to the correct address or with the correct filing fees.

However, if you are submitting forms that have a filing deadline, such as for an appeal or a request for evidence, you should take extra care to mail your package to the correct address and to include the correct filing fee. Failure to do so could result in missing the filing deadline, an issue that can be difficult or impossible to correct.

Immigration Mistake 13
Failing to keep copies of all immigration related documents.

You should always keep copies of every document or form related to your immigration status. This includes a copy of your visa application, all pages of your passport including any visas or stamps in it, your I-94 card, any notices you receive from the government related to your immigration status, and copies of any other immigration related application you submit (including copies of any supporting evidence submitted with the government forms). If you are ever in immigration court proceedings, you should keep copies of all the notices related to your case, any documents that are filed with the court by your attorney or the government attorney and copies of any orders of the immigration judge.

It is not uncommon to need these documents years later for future immigration applications, immigration court proceedings or for immigration appeals. If you lose your copies of these documents, it may be a very time consuming and expensive process to get replacements. Depending on your situation, you may not have the time to wait six months to a year to get replacements from the government files. In addition, if you need to work with an immigration lawyer on an immigration court case or an immigration appeal, the lawyer will likely need to review these documents before being able to determine the best course of action in your case.

To avoid future frustrations and unnecessary expenses, always keep copies of any paperwork related to your immigration status.

Immigration Mistake 14
Failing to keep records that may be needed for future immigration applications.

Failing to keep records that may be needed for future immigration applications is a common mistake that is closely related to failing to keep copies of your immigration related documents. Many types of immigration applications require you to present evidence that proves you are eligible for the benefit that you are seeking.

For example, if you are filing an application to adjust status and become a permanent resident based on your marriage to a United States citizen, you will need to present a certified copy of your birth certificate, your marriage certificate and any divorce decrees of you or your spouse. You will also need to show proof of your immigration status, including evidence of how you entered the United States. Many other immigration applications require similar types of evidence. You should keep copies of all of these important documents in a safe location so that you can easily submit them if needed for a future application.

Another example of the importance of keeping records for immigration purposes involves the evidence needed to file for cancellation of removal. If you are not a permanent resident and have been in the United States for over ten years, you may be eligible to file an application for cancellation of removal if you are ever placed in deportation proceedings. One of the requirements for this type of relief is that you prove that you have continuously resided in the United States for ten years. It is not enough to show that you entered the United States ten years ago. You must present evidence from the entire ten year time period that will prove that you were in the United States. This evidence can include such items as tax records, employment records, school records of yourself or your children, medical records, photographs, etc.

The reality is that most people simply don't keep records going back ten years. However, if you are in a situation where you may someday need to apply for cancellation of removal, you should take care to keep records that go back at least ten years. You shouldn't wait until you find yourself in immigration court proceedings to start collecting these documents because at that time they may no longer be available or you may not be able to collect them in time for your hearing.

Immigration Mistake 15
Not submitting the evidence required to win your case.

You won't win your case if you don't submit the evidence needed to win. Most people who don't submit the evidence needed fail to do so because they simply don't know what evidence they need to submit. Immigration law is complicated and it isn't always easy to figure out what evidence is needed to win. As difficult as it can be to sort through the immigration regulations and instructions, it is essential that you do so before you submit your immigration application or attend your immigration court hearing.

Depending on the situation, if you don't submit the required evidence, you may automatically lose your case. You may not be able to simply appeal your case and submit additional evidence as part of your appeal. For example, in an appeal from a decision of an immigration judge, you are not allowed to submit any new evidence that wasn't submitted at the immigration court hearing. This means that your appeal may be impossible to win if the correct evidence wasn't submitted during the immigration court proceedings. I can't stress enough how important it is to make sure that you understand what evidence needs to be submitted and when it needs to be submitted. Failing to follow the rules concerning submitting evidence can result in immigration problems that simply can't be fixed.

When submitting evidence as part of an immigration application to USCIS, it is important that you present the evidence so the reviewer can understand it. It is not the reviewer's job to piece the evidence together to see whether your application should be approved. It is your job to show the reviewer that you qualify and to make it easy for the reviewer to see that you qualify. Don't just throw your evidence into an envelope and hope the reviewer will figure it out. The evidence you submit should be organized and in some cases you should include a legal memo that explains to the reviewer why your application should be approved.

Finally, you should always make sure to submit translations of any documents that are not in English, along with a translator's certificate. Documents that don't have an English translation will not be considered in reviewing your application.

❖ ❖ ❖

HOW CAN AN IMMIGRATION LAWYER HELP YOU?

You should not hire an immigration lawyer to simply fill out forms for you. Although your immigration lawyer will normally prepare any required forms for you, the primary role of your immigration lawyer should be in providing you with legal advice, identifying legal issues, researching and drafting legal briefs (if needed for your case) and representing you at immigration interviews or hearings.

Immigration Court Proceedings or Asylum Hearings

In immigration court proceedings or asylum hearings, your immigration lawyer can help you by: identifying the forms of relief for which you qualify, identifying the required evidence needed for each form of relief, helping to obtain expert testimony if required, preparing you for your hearing, drafting and filing court documents such as motions and legal briefs, and conducting direct and cross-examination of witnesses during your hearing.

Identifying the forms of relief for which you qualify. Depending on your situation, you may be eligible for one or more forms of relief from removal. An immigration lawyer can help you identify each form of relief for which you qualify and can help you evaluate which options provide you with the best chance of success.

Identifying the required evidence needed for each form of relief. The success of your asylum claim or application for relief from removal will depend largely on the evidence that you present and whether that evidence is found to be credible Your immigration lawyer will help you identify the evidence needed to support your asylum claim or application for relief from removal. In addition, your immigration lawyer will be able to present your evidence in a clear, organized manner that will support a finding of credibility by the immigration judge.

Helping to obtain expert testimony if needed. Depending on the nature of your case, you may need to present expert testimony in order to win. This is particularly true for some asylum claims or in cases where you need to prove the conditions in your home country. Expert testimony can also include medical experts that can testify about the physical and mental effects of the persecution or abuse that you suffered in the past. Your immigration lawyer can help you identify whether such expert testimony is needed in your case and can identify appropriate experts to testify on your behalf.

Preparing you for your hearing. Your immigration lawyer will help you prepare for each of your immigration hearings. For your initial hearing (called a master calendar hearing), your lawyer will be able to explain to you what will happen during the hearing and will be able to help you determine the best way for you to plead to the allegations against you. For your individual merits hearing where you will present your case to the immigration judge, your lawyer will help you prepare to testify in court. Depending on the nature of your case, your lawyer may do a mock hearing so that you can practice answering questions about your case before your hearing. Your lawyer will also be able to explain to you what types of questions you should expect to be asked by the immigration judge and the government's lawyer.

Drafting and filing court documents, including motions and legal briefs. Most immigration court cases will involve drafting and filing documents with the court, including legal motions and legal briefs. These are technical legal documents. It can be very difficult to draft these documents correctly if you do not have legal training. Your lawyer will prepare these documents for you and will file them with the court in the proper way.

Asking questions during your hearing. Many cases in immigration court will require that you and your witnesses testify during the hearing. Your lawyer will ask you and your witnesses questions designed to address all of the legal elements required for you to win your case. After your lawyer asks you questions, the government's lawyer will be allowed to ask you questions. Your lawyer will be able to object to any inappropriate questions that the government's lawyer asks you. After the government's lawyer finishes asking you questions, your lawyer will then have the opportunity to ask you additional questions if anything needs to be clarified.

In the event that the government calls witnesses to testify against you, your lawyer will be able to ask the government's witnesses questions as well.

Unless you know exactly what needs to be proven in order to win your case and you are familiar with the rules that control how you can ask questions during the hearing, you likely will find it very difficult to do this on your own.

Immigration Benefits Applications

If you are applying for an immigration benefit, such as a visa, status as a permanent resident or naturalization, your immigration lawyer can help you successfully navigate the application process. Your lawyer can also assist you in minimizing the risk of future immigration problems. Your lawyer will be able to help you by: identifying the legal issues that could potentially result in your being placed in deportation proceedings, verifying that you meet all the requirements before you submit your application, identifying and evaluating all possible immigration options that you may have, evaluating whether past criminal convictions will cause future immigration problems or make you inadmissible to the United States, and assisting you with preparing and filing your immigration applications.

Identifying the legal issues that could potentially result in your being placed in deportation proceedings. Before you submit an application for an immigration benefit, your lawyer will review the legal issues that could create problems for your case. After reviewing your case, your lawyer will then be able to provide you with an assessment of the risks associated with your application. In particular, your lawyer will be able to let you know if there is a risk that you will be placed in deportation proceedings as a result of the application

Verifying that you meet all the requirements before you submit your application. In some cases, it may not be clear if you meet all of the requirements for the immigration benefit for which you are applying. If you don't qualify, your application will be denied and your filing fee will not be refunded. Because the filing fees for immigration applications can cost hundreds if not thousands of dollars, your lawyer will help you verify that you meet the basic eligibility requirements before you pay the filing fee.

Identifying and evaluating all possible immigration options that you may have. Your immigration lawyer will help you identify each immigration option that may allow you to achieve your goals. Depending on your situation, you may have more than one option that you could pursue. Your lawyer will help you to determine which option would be the best for you and whether you should pursue more than one option at the same time.

Evaluating whether your criminal convictions will cause future immigration problems or make you inadmissible to the United States. Many criminal convictions can create serious immigration consequences. If you have any type of criminal conviction -- even if the conviction was expunged or you were given an alternative sentencing or diversion program -- you should let your immigration lawyer know about the conviction. Your lawyer will likely want to review the criminal court records to identify what immigration consequences you may face and if there is any way to minimize or eliminate those consequences.

The best time to do this type of evaluation is before you accept a plea bargain or go to trial in a criminal court. But, if your criminal court case is already completed, you should consult with an immigration lawyer as soon as possible to that you can better understand how the criminal court case may affect your future immigration options.

Assisting you with preparing and filing your immigration applications. Your immigration lawyer will also assist you with preparing and filing your immigration applications. This will include completing all of the necessary forms correctly as well as presenting the necessary supporting evidence in a way that makes it easy for the immigration officer who reviews the package to see that your application should be approved.

❖ ❖ ❖

HOW TO HIRE AN IMMIGRATION LAWYER

Choosing a lawyer to represent you is obviously an important task. The task of choosing an immigration lawyer for your immigration case is complicated by the fact that there are many areas of immigration law. Some lawyers will specialize in business or employment immigration issues. Others will specialize in cases involving litigation such as immigration court hearings or immigration appeals. Among lawyers who accept immigration court cases, not all will accept cases that involve asylum applications or that involve people who are in immigration detention. Some lawyers who accept family immigration cases may not accept family immigration cases where waivers are required. A good starting point in hiring an immigration lawyer is to check whether the lawyer accepts cases like yours.

The decision of which lawyer to hire certainly should not be made on the basis of advertising alone. The Yellow Pages and Craigslist are filled with ads – all of which say basically the same thing. You should not hire based solely on advertising. You shouldn't even hire me until you trust that I can do a good job for you.

You also cannot rely solely on the recommendations of friends and family. The fact that a lawyer did a good job on a friend's DWI case or a relative's divorce does not make him the best lawyer for your immigration law case. Immigration law is very complex. Just because a lawyer is very skilled in another area of law does not make that lawyer the best choice for your immigration case. Likewise, just because a lawyer did a good job with your friend's employment-based immigration case does not make the lawyer the best choice for your asylum case. I cannot say it too often: immigration matters are different and difficult.

You should also be careful of relying solely on "directories" of lawyers, especially those claiming to list the "best" or "top" lawyers or those that provide lawyer rankings. If the directory doesn't tell you exactly how they select the "best" lawyers or how they rank lawyers, how do you know that the rankings reflect what is important to your case? After all, is a lawyer the "best" simply because they paid to be included in the directory? If the rankings give weight to the number of academic articles that a lawyer has published, is that important to you if you need someone to argue your case in court? You should be careful to avoid blindly relying on the rankings that other people put together unless you know that those rankings reflect what is important to you.

This does not mean that you should simply ignore directory listings or referral services. You should just be wary of relying on rankings provided by others unless the person doing the ranking can describe how they came up with the rankings and you are confident that the rankings reflect what is important to you. General directory services can be a useful tool in helping you identify immigration lawyers in your area that you may want to add to your initial list of lawyers to contact. You should also add to your list the lawyers who are recommended to you by friends and family and the lawyers you identify through your own research, including Internet searches.

Which immigration lawyer is best for you?

How do you find out which lawyer is the best in your area for your case? I believe that there are key questions to ask that will help you find the best lawyer for your immigration case. It will involve some time on your part, but that's a fair price to pay.

The "best" immigration lawyer for you will depend on many things, including your personal preferences and the immigration issue you have. Some of the factors that you should consider are discussed below. These factors are not in any particular order because what is important to one person may not be important to another. The items discussed below, however, should give you a good starting point in deciding which immigration lawyer is best for you.

Consultation policy. I've found that many people who call my office ask about my consultation policy before they ask about anything else. If you are choosing an immigration lawyer based on the lawyer's consultation policy, you should make sure that you understand what the lawyer means by a consultation.

For example, some lawyers will offer a free phone consultation. Others will offer free office consultations. Others will charge a fee for consultations. The choice that each lawyer makes is based on many issues and all the above options are valid options.

The most important thing to keep in mind is the purpose of the consultation. Your primary goal in a legal consultation should be to identify whether the lawyer is a good match for you and your immigration case. You should not expect an immigration lawyer to be able to provide you with detailed legal advice during a legal consultation, especially if the consultation is short or your issues are complex. As discussed above, immigration issues are complex. You should not be surprised if a lawyer needs to take a closer look at your case before providing you with legal advice.

You should use the consultation to decide if you would feel comfortable working with the lawyer. You should also use the consultation to see if the lawyer can describe immigration options to you in a way that you can understand. In many cases, the lawyer may also be able to identify the options that should be explored in your case and how the lawyer would go about identifying the best option for you.

Location of office. Depending on your situation, the location of the lawyer's office may also be an important factor in deciding which immigration lawyer is best for you.

For example, if you live in Norfolk, Virginia and are placed in immigration court proceedings, your case will likely be at the Arlington Immigration Court in Arlington, Virginia. Would it be better to hire an immigration lawyer in the Norfolk area or one in the Arlington area? The Norfolk lawyer would have the benefit of being closer to where you live so that it would be easier for you to have face-to-face meetings to discuss your case. The disadvantage is that the lawyer's fees may be higher to account for the added travel time that the lawyer will spend in order to go to the Arlington Immigration Court to represent you.

An immigration lawyer located closer to the Arlington Immigration Court may be able to offer you a more affordable attorney fee because there will not be as much time spent traveling to the court for your hearings. But, if you are not comfortable with working with your attorney on a long distance basis, this may not be a workable option for you. You should carefully consider whether you would be comfortable working with your attorney via phone and email and whether you would be able to travel to their office for any meetings.

On the other hand, many family-based immigration petitions involve issues that are not as complex as immigration court cases. If your case does not have any special issues, you may feel comfortable working with a lawyer who is located far from you and communicating solely by phone or email. If your case involves having to go to an interview at your local USCIS office, you should consider whether you would be comfortable going to the interview on your own without your lawyer. A local lawyer will more easily be able to attend your interview with you compared to a lawyer who is located far away.

Location can also be an issue when choosing between lawyers located in your local geographic area. If you don't have access to a car, is the lawyer's office conveniently located to public transportation? If you will only be able to take short breaks from work in order to meet with your lawyer, is the lawyer's office located close to your office? Is the lawyer such a good match in every other way that you don't mind having a longer drive to get to the lawyer's office?

Personality. It is not uncommon for immigration matters to take months or years to resolve. With this in mind, you should consider whether the immigration lawyer is a good personality match for you. After all, you probably don't want to spend months or years working with someone who you simply don't like to be around!

Does the lawyer explain so that you can understand? As mentioned elsewhere in this book, immigration law is very complex. Does the lawyer explain the issues important to your case so that you can understand them? The odds are that whatever the issue is, if it is important to your case, you'll want to understand it so that you can make good decisions about your case.

Lawyer's fee. Most likely, the lawyer's fee will also be a factor in deciding which lawyer is the best one for you. Key items related to the lawyer's fee that you should consider are: value, affordability, payment plans and whether the lawyer accepts the form of payment you want to use such as credit cards.

The value of a lawyer's fee should be an important consideration, but you should avoid using the lawyer's fee as your sole basis for hiring a lawyer. This means that you should not simply shop around for the lawyer with the lowest fees, nor should you assume that the lawyer with the highest fees is the best one for you. Instead, you should consider the overall value that is being offered. What is included with the fee? Will you be charged extra for phone calls, online legal research or postage? Will the lawyer attend your interview with you or would an additional fee be charged? Will you be charged extra if the government requests additional information in your case? Are you confident in the lawyer's ability to represent you?

Although the lawyer's fee should not be your sole basis for hiring a lawyer, the overall affordability of the lawyer should be considered. After all, if the lawyer's fee does not fit within your budget, you may want to continue your search for a lawyer. You may also want to check to see if the lawyer offers payment plans or alternative forms of payment such as credit cards that may allow you to more easily fit the lawyer's fee within your budget.

Language barrier. You should keep in mind that English is the language that will be used to communicate with USCIS and the immigration court. Therefore, your lawyer's ability to effectively communicate in English should be the most important language issue when hiring an immigration lawyer.

At the same time, you should feel comfortable in communicating with your lawyer. If your native language is not English, how important is it to you that your immigration lawyer speaks your native language? If you are not comfortable discussing your case in English and the lawyer doesn't know your native language, would you be comfortable working with a translator? Does the lawyer have someone in their office who can translate or do you have a friend who would be willing to help translate? There are no right or wrong answers to these questions --- the important thing is that you are comfortable working with your lawyer.

Large or small law firm. This is another area where there is no one right answer --- what you are comfortable with is what is important. A smaller law firm may be able to provide you with the ability to work directly with your lawyer instead of working through a paralegal or case manager. You should consider how important it is to you to always have direct access to your lawyer or if you are willing to work with a paralegal or case manager in addition to your lawyer.

A larger law firm, however, may be able to respond to your questions more quickly because they have a larger staff that can answer questions. For example, I am the only lawyer at my firm. If a client calls with a question when I am in court, my client would have to wait until I am out of court to receive an answer. A larger law firm may be able to have someone else at the firm provide an immediate answer. On the other hand, my clients know that when they hire me that I will be the person that they will be working with and that they will have direct access to me.

Membership in professional organizations. Because immigration law is constantly changing, it is important that you hire an immigration lawyer who keeps up with the changes in the law. One of the best ways for a lawyer to do this is to join a professional organization such as the American Immigration Lawyers Association (AILA). AILA is a national association of over 11,000 lawyers and law professors who practice and teach immigration law. Among other things, AILA provides continuing legal education and information that helps its members stay up to date with new developments in immigration law. I am a member of AILA and receive daily updates of new developments in immigration law. These updates help me to ensure that my clients are not surprised by any new developments in the law. If your lawyer is not a member of AILA, you should ask them what steps they take to keep up to date with changes in immigration law.

Many types of immigration law. Immigration law is a very big field and not all immigration lawyers handle all types of immigration cases. For example, some lawyers only handle employment immigration cases. Others only handle family based immigration cases. Many immigration lawyers do not accept cases that involve representing people in immigration court. When trying to locate the best immigration lawyer for you, you should always check to see if the lawyer handles your type of immigration case. After all, a lawyer who only handles employment immigration cases may not be the best choice for your asylum case.

Special issue for cases involving immigration detention. If you are hiring a lawyer to represent someone in immigration detention, you should verify whether the lawyer accepts cases involving someone who is detained. Just as not all lawyers accept cases involving representation in immigration court, not all lawyers who accept immigration court cases will accept cases where a person is in immigration detention.

Willing to provide general information. Is the lawyer willing to provide you with some general information before you hire them to help you decide whether the lawyer is a good match for you? As discussed above, you should feel comfortable that the lawyer can do a good job for you, is a good personality match for you and can explain things in a way that you can understand. You should check to see if the lawyer is willing to provide you with some general information so that you can get a better feel for whether the lawyer is a good match for you in these areas. You also should check to see if the lawyer's website or blog provide you with information that helps you evaluate whether the lawyer is a good match for you. Does the lawyer have any materials, such as this book, that you can read before you hire the lawyer to get a better feel for who the lawyer is?

Is the lawyer willing to explain at your initial meeting the basic issues in your case and how they would proceed to handle your case before you commit to hiring the lawyer? Keep in mind that there is a difference between providing general information and specific legal advice. It is reasonable to ask a lawyer to provide general information or to summarize the steps they would take identify the best course of action for your case. But, you should not expect to receive legal advice specific to your situation until you have hired the lawyer and the lawyer has had the opportunity to really learn the details of your case.

❖ ❖ ❖

ABOUT THE AUTHOR

When people ask me what I do, I often tell them that "I help future Americans become citizens." The goal of almost all of my clients is to be able to someday become United States citizens, and I help them achieve that goal.

As an immigration lawyer I represent people who need assistance with immigration court proceedings, asylum applications, family-based immigration petitions, marriage-based immigration petitions, naturalization applications and immigration appeals. In particular, I accept cases where people need representation at the Arlington Immigration Court, the Baltimore Immigration Court, the Arlington Asylum Office, the Board of Immigration Appeals, the USCIS Washington Field Office (located in Fairfax, Virginia), or the USCIS Baltimore office.

You can learn more about my immigration law practice by visiting my websites:

http://www.kschaeferlaw.com

and

http://www.dc-immigration-blog.com

These websites are intended to provide additional up to date information on immigration law issues. In particular, my immigration blog at http://www.dc-immigration-blog.com is designed to provide general information about immigration related issues and to help my clients stay up to date on changes in immigration law.

I initially became interested in immigration law while completing intensive consular officer training offered by the

Department of State at the National Foreign Affairs Training Center in Arlington, Virginia. My interest in immigration law deepened while providing consular services in Lagos, Nigeria. I have an international background and have lived or worked in the United States, Europe, Asia and Africa. I am a member of the American Immigration Lawyers Association (AILA).

I am a graduate of Georgetown University Law Center where I graduated *magna cum laude* and was awarded the Order of the Coif honor in recognition of graduating in the top 10% of my law school class. While in law school I served as the Notes Development Editor of the American Criminal Law Review. Prior to attending law school I served as a communications officer in the United States Marine Corps and worked in both private and public sectors.

I am licensed to practice law in the District of Columbia and am admitted to practice in the District of Columbia courts and the District Court of the District of Columbia federal court. My practice outside of the District of Columbia is limited to immigration and nationality law.

❖ ❖ ❖

ABOUT THE SCHAEFER LAW FIRM

The main office of the Schaefer Law Firm office is located in the Farragut Square area of the District of Columbia, near the corner of Connecticut and K Street NW. The street address is:

1629 K Street NW, Suite 300
Washington, DC 20006

There is plenty of public parking in the area.

The office is also conveniently located near two Metro stations. It is approximately one block from the Farragut North Metro Station serviced by the Red Line and is less than two blocks from the Farragut West Metro Station serviced by the Orange Line and Blue Line. Other public transportation options include Metrobus and the nearby bus lines include the L2, L4, S2 and S4 lines.

Clients can also schedule meetings at the firm's office located in Northern Virginia at the Reston Town Center. This office is conveniently located near the Reston Avenue exit on the Dulles Toll Road. The street address is:

1818 Library Street, Suite 500
Reston, VA 20190

There are several free public parking garages located at the Reston Town Center.

❖ ❖ ❖

NOTES

NOTES

NOTES

NOTES

NOTES